Cultural Heritage Map

poems by

D. G. Geis

Finishing Line Press
Georgetown, Kentucky

Cultural Heritage Map

Copyright © 2018 by D. G. Geis
ISBN 978-1-63534-716-6 First Edition
All rights reserved under International and Pan-American Copyright Conventions. No part of this book may be reproduced in any manner whatsoever without written permission from the publisher, except in the case of brief quotations embodied in critical articles and reviews.

ACKNOWLEDGMENTS

Grateful acknowledgement is made to the following publications in which some of these poems first appeared:

"Marriage" in *The Moth* (also reprinted *The Irish Times*)
"Visit To A Small Planet" in *Prime Number*
"Magic" in *The Galway Review* (Ireland)
"Why I read the *National Enquirer*" in *Skylight 47* (Ireland)
"Mockumentary" in *The Broadkill Review*
"Ask a tattooist about true love" in *Crannog Magazine* (Ireland)
"Cultural Heritage Map" in *Magnolia Review*
"What the Handcart Said to the Tollbooth Attendant" and "If a human body falls" in *Forage*
"Mad Science" in *Masque and Spectacle*
"Cenotaph" in *The Broad River Review*
"Jamaican Honeymoon" in *Fjords*
"If Cowboys Were Cancer Cells" in *Crab Creek Review*
"To Li Po pissing on the rainbow" in *A New Ulster Review* (N. Ireland)
"A Stockyard Liturgy" in *The Tishman Review*
"Psalm 152" in *The Naugatuck River Review*

Publisher: Leah Maines
Editor: Christen Kincaid
Cover Art: D. G. Geis
Author Photo: D. G. Geis
Cover Design: Elizabeth Maines McCleavy

Printed in the USA on acid-free paper.
Order online: www.finishinglinepress.com
also available on amazon.com

Author inquiries and mail orders:
Finishing Line Press
P. O. Box 1626
Georgetown, Kentucky 40324
U. S. A.

Table of Contents

Marriage 1

Visit To A Small Planet 3

Magic 5

Why I Read *The National Enquirer* 6

Mockumentary 7

Ask A Tattooist 8

Cultural Heritage Map 10

What The Handcart Said To The Tollbooth Attendant 11

Cenotaph 13

Cowboys Were Cancer Cells 16

Elegy For Jan Marejko 18

If A Human Body Falls 20

Mad Science 21

To Li Po Pissing on the Rainbow 23

A Stockyard Liturgy 25

Ask Marilyn 26

Missionary Stew 28

Psalm 152 29

A Hangover With Emily D 33

For Noah

Marriage

Montaigne compared it
to a birdcage.

Socrates claimed a bad one
made you a philosopher.

Luther prayed the conjugal rose
would open nightly

and believed the marriage bed
a "school for character".

Luther's paradise
proved too heavenly

for postdiluvians
still clinging to their mattresses

as the waters ebbed.
And did Adam,

the first husband,
know that as he hardened

his resolve
and Eve, the first wife,

spread her legs,
creation also moaned?

Or the wolves that howled
when they received their names

would become the dogs
to wag the tail

end of domesticity;
dogs whose days span further

than most marriages
and whose ignorance

knows nothing
of such bliss—

yet still answer
to their names.

That two humans
thrown together by chance

are called spouses.
Or a flock of ravens,

an unkindness.

Visit to a Small Planet

No telling
what He thinks—or if.

His ears,
a zillion light years wide,

pressed to the fizzy heart
of the universe,

a hydrogen gasbag
folded in on itself

like table napkins
on the Hindenburg,

an omelet,
or a quantum quesadilla.

What we call spiral galaxies,
He calls soup and sandwiches.

What we call supernovas,
He calls shoe polish.

What we call black holes,
He calls a paycheck.

What we call space,
He calls the barstool.

What we call the Big Bang,
He calls Louise.

It's why the sun's
so hysterical

and the moon
so matter of fact.

But it's also why
stars twinkle—

The Big Guy winking at us,
humming a little tune

to Himself,
while he helps Louise

with her zipper.

Magic

This sleight of hand
called life—

the wives
we make disappear

and children
we pull out of hats.

The parents who, over time,
we saw painlessly in half

and the complicated knots
that untie themselves.

The doves and serpents
pulled from Jehovah's empty sleeve

to misdirect
the mischief of our making:

the compassion we feel
for a rag in the road

believing it to be
a squashed puppy.

Or the cock killed for Asclepius
to thank Houdini God,

our Chained Magician
drowning

in his locked box.

Why I Read *The National Enquirer*

Because I believe in the gods
and the inexorability of divine things.

That Zeus is an impenitent philanderer
with a zigzag cock, nicknamed "Thunderbolt",

and that before he knocked up Hera,
she was a lap dancer at the Olympus Club.

That Dionysius was spotted partying
in Athens his first day out of rehab.

That Hermes cheated on his taxes and
has a new reality show called "Life on the Inside".

That Apollo is a sex addict
with a 500 drachma a day cocaine habit.

That Charon is losing money hand over fist
to unlicensed ferrymen.

That Ares is halfway through his sex change
and has checked into a hospital in Corinth for the final cut.

That Pan was arrested in Delos
for failure to register as a sex offender.

That Demeter is gluten intolerant.
And that Aphrodite

bending over in a micro-mini
and a pair of Jimmy Choo stilettos

would rock just about any world.

Mockumentary

Count the leashed dogs
pulling homeowners

down the sidewalk
or the neighborly oaks lining up

to shake hands across the street,
the garbage truck

stumbling down Del Monte
with all the lives, neatly bagged,

crushed in the back.
And don't forget Mr. Sun,

the bright eyed prosecutor,
rising to make his case,

the "For Sale" signs
further down the road,

and the mailman
in his light blue uniform,

efficient as always,
delivering this, Dear Resident,

your final offer.

Ask a tattooist

about true love—

all the Suzannes
smothered under Yin-Yangs

or Michaels devoured
by butterflies;

the Karens lasered off
with no more consideration

than bacon frying in a pan.
Or the Jasons

now stamped VOID,
as superfluous as a bounced check.

Ask a tattooist
about the fickleness of human nature,

the irresolution of erasure,
and the palimpsest of regret.

That the tendency of ink
is to waver enduringly

and the word made flesh
to deliquesce.

How everything reckoned
to a certainty

can so easily
be crossed out;

everything, that is,
except your birthmark.

About which he informs you,
regrettably—

nothing can be done.

Cultural Heritage Map

It is Bach's B Minor Mass.

It is Pol Pot's library card.

It is the invention of painless dentistry.

It is the wreck of the *Andrea Doria*.

It is Washoe signing "Tickle me!"

It is John Wayne Gacy signing an autograph.

It is Albrecht Durer's woodcuts.

It is a stripper named Pandora.

It is Jesus in *The Sermon On The Mount*.

It is Walmart cashiers wearing surgical gloves.

It is Thomas Mann in Hollywood.

It is Liberace in Vegas.

It is a Boy Scout merit badge.

It is the Amalekites.

It is a color illustration from *The Watchtower* of Jehovah's Witnesses picnicking in heaven.

It is *The Mendoza Codex* with an Aztec priest holding a heart in his hand.

It is *The Venus of Willendorf*.

It is Mr. Potato Head.

What the Handcart Said to the Tollbooth Attendant

My wife remembers growing up in Old Beirut
where there was an ice skating rink
in the basement of the *Bristol Hotel*
and Sister Grazia of the *Italian Girl's School*
warned them about the special dangers
of Italian boys and drinking too much beer.

Muslim, Christian, Druze, Jew,
all skated merrily on the same thin ice,
shaved so tenderly by the only *Zamboni*
in the Levant.
There were daytime shopping trips
to Damascus for table linens,
surfing south of Beirut,
and the good guys all spoke French.

History has other ironies, of course:
Sergeant John C. Woods,
"The Hangman of Nuremeburg",
accidentally electrocuted
while repairing a power line in 1950;
Sir Laurence Olivier demanding
on his deathbed to watch *The Simpsons;*
and tourists taking selfies at Auschwitz.

But because there's more to life
than Holocaust Museums,
I've decided to leave Hell behind
and return to Paradise,
a world as improbable
as a bleeding oyster
or a free sample pack of catheters.

A world in which the sun rises
only to swagger across the heavens,
drafting behind God's wheelchair,
while the rest of us loll expectantly
in the cellphone parking lot—
and the only question
worth answering is:
"If I was a beggar,
what would my sign say?"

O ye of little faith,
do free range chickens
really meet a better end?

In *Gunsmoke*, when Miss Kitty
took a cowboy upstairs,

everyone knew where they were going.

Cenotaph

When I consider
the suffering

that life occasions,
I remember the stars.

How badly they must sleep
to turn continuously

in their vast beds.
The gratitude they must feel

to have given themselves
so completely—

and finally collapse
in heaven's arms.

How when their fever breaks
and the light goes out of them,

the light still reaches us;
and that what we see

is not the star itself,
but its memorial,

a luminous confession
of what is no longer there.

And while we worship the light,
the stars themselves

prefer to reverence darkness,
for whom distance is love;

and endless praise,
a canticle to emptiness.
Jamaican Honeymoon

Tomorrow your footprints will be raked clean,
But today you are floating in the pool
With a frozen Pina Colada.

The pool waiters babble in patwa
While on the balcony a grackle pecks indignantly
At your remaindered breakfast.

Too much bagel, not enough toast.
The bluebird of happiness has darkened considerably,
Prefers champagne to rum, and wants you to know.

Your schedule today is severe:
History in the morning; Nature in the afternoon.
The Tour of Life here runs in reverse.

You will visit the Anglican Church of St. James
(Once the slave's hospital). And later see the vault
Where the slaves burned Massa's money—

And the cottonwood tree
Where the slaves were hanged.
No, you will not save the dolphins.

But while snorkeling at a meet and greet,
One frisky bull will hump your leg.
No sea urchins will give you a wedding gift

And the pedicurist knows all the
Ins and outs of pruning *Jefe's* feet.
You will survive the couple's scavenger hunt,

Drain martinis with a plasterer
From New Jersey, and sing one too many
Choruses at the piano bar.

Stumble graciously beneath the upturned palms
And pee merrily under the stars before dawn's
Curly light greets you with its rosy hammer.

Your hangover will not go out with the tide,
But over dry toast you will follow the wiggling
Backside of a bridesmaid, jogging on the beach,

Powering up for her first Sunrise of the day.
Poolside, the ponytailed nonagenarian
From Cleveland will be attended to

So sweetly by his nursing Rasta queen.
And as Ackee trees bow down to meet you,
Peacocks will strut among the fancy deck chairs.

Such Paradise! A garden where Jah
Lets animals name themselves.
And the Ark never loses sight of land.

This trebled martini of a heaven,
A kingdom peaceable, where The Help
Speak in tongues with words

Which passeth all understanding.
Though what you hear is not for you to say.
It is Almighty Jah

Whispering to his sunburned children.
And the language He is speaking
Is the language of slaves.

If Cowboys Were Cancer Cells

They'd be driving
a herd through town

on their way
to the railhead at Lourdes,

smashing up saloons,
whoring night and day

in the brothel of your innards,
running their cattle

up and down Main Street
through the swinging doors

of your lymph nodes.
Frightening all the decent folks,

waving their guns around,
riding roughshod

over your immune system.
Rowdy bastards

and ingrates to boot.
After everything

you've given them,
you'd think they'd let up:

the bullying,
the peace they've disturbed,

all the good women they've ruined,
the long shadows they've cast.

And your inner Yul Brynner
ready to go down

with both barrels blazing.
High Noon with a drip bag.

And a gap-toothed *bandido*
looking a lot like Eli Wallach

hamming it up,
telling you that if God

hadn't wanted you sheared,
He wouldn't have made

you sheep.

Elegy for Jan Marejko
For Tessa and Samantha

We chased cows in the *Saleve*
and laughed at *les zombies* in Geneva.
Nietzsche loved cows, you said.
But I think it was just the cowbells
you loved to hear, skittish Brahmans
ringing a lovelorn terrorist's
hours of prayer.
When we were young
you once told me
that the worst hauntings
were by happy ghosts—
as if after 35 years, death's sting
would still be good for a laugh.
And I agree with you
that there is nothing better
in this sad world
than to be the *Bichon Frise*
of a dowager in Zurich.
Though I fear
you never really had enough
of life to let it go,
the old dog did have a new trick.
And rascal that you were,
you managed to slip your leash.
You and your lucky Swiss passport,
able to leap tall borders
in a single bound;
though what border guard
would stop you now?
Herr Doktor Refugee,
a citizen of everywhere
and nowhere, holed up now
in his mahogany *Pensione*,
sleeping one off,
the earth pulled up over your head
like a down comforter.

How hard it is to rise in the morning,
you used to tell me.
And how the light hurt your eyes!
Was *terra firma* ever less firm
or your intentions more clear?
You stopped the world. You got off.
Though even now, your heart slips
through my hands like a soapy baby.
How should I weigh your choosing?
You who chose otherwise.
You who saw Nothing
and embraced it with a full stop,
yet missed the final blessing:

to see that we are nothing,
and *not* to die—

but rejoice.

If a human body falls from the top of the Empire State Building does it explode or remain intact?

A question not
to be entertained lightly.

Considering the terminal velocity
of mortal flesh,

its tendency to fall
at a constant rate,

and upon rare occasion
to bloom substantially.

To wake sleeping history
with a final jolt.

And grace the cover of Life—
refused in its entirety

by Miss Evelyn McHale
as she struck a limousine

from 86 stories up.
A confectioned angel

colorized in repose,
leaping from Observation

Deck to warranted conclusion,
a transaction both satisfying and complete:

that death is an abstraction
consummated only

by the concrete.

Mad Science

How far we've paddled
from *Ye Olde Tidal Pool!*

Between the shark liver oil
in *Preparation H*

and *eau de vie* of *Cnidaria*
in *Prevagen*,

we soldier on.
Life's stinging tentacles

defused,
the world's our oyster.

And fins forgotten,
we've landed on our feet.

From top to bottom,
our memories jogged,

our troubled wrinkles stilled,
we gimp gamely

into a future
where even The Heavens

declare the non-event of
our passing—

And as we make
our unhurried transition

from ashes to diamonds
or dust to eco-friendly planters,

we wave goodbye,
a final act of attrition

to commemorate our timely dispersal.
A castaway's *hallelujah*!

at the sighting
of death's black sails.

To leave a bauble
for our bubble

at the check-out counter
of this cosmic dollar store

and pennies on the dollar,
pledge our depleted atoms

at The Heavenly Pawnshop;
to be redeemed or rearranged—

whichever the hell comes first.

To Li Po Pissing on the Rainbow

O Li Po—

I read you when I'm sad
or buzzed

and need to hide
like smokers in Pompeii

after Vesuvius
molded them into ashtrays.

The tip of my e-cig
glows white

and my new Cadillac
has lane assist.

Screw smoking.
Even driving drunk is safer now!

So forget about
embracing your reflection

on the river's moonlit face.
Those days are gone.

Now our empty mirror
is a selfie stick.

For this bedraggled old Buddha,
time drizzles

on the windshield of life
as water in the gutter

sparkles so cleanly
on its long way home

through the storm sewers,
winding underground

to the sea.

A Stockyard Liturgy
    For Temple Grandin

O Lord—
If history is a slaughterhouse,

May our paths always curve
And be trod without diversion.

Let no sharp angle impede our progress
Or uncertainty give us pause.

Permit us to stream freely
Down the conveyer

And grant us one final hug
Before we are stunned.

As blood flows freely
Along the path

Of least resistance,
So may the meat hook

Of inevitability
Lift us high above all butchery,

And our ending,
God willing—

Be both sudden
And humane.

Ask Marilyn

*"If you're wondering
if you're dreaming;
you're dreaming."*
Marilyn vos Savant

You are genius on Parade.
Even your name states the case;
as axiomatic as arithmetic or the flu.

Every Sunday the Oracle speaks.
Pythia, High Priestess of Apollo,
peddling truth to *hausfraus*

and the clueless from the temple
of stretch pants, salad shooters,
and collector's dachshund mugs.

Wisdom midwifed
in the marketplace of what passes
these days for Athens.

And though Socrates
might have a word to say
about the downside of truth-telling

or the relevance of the popular vote,
who knows whether the world's navel
passes through the lobby

of a Day's Inn in Cleveland
or what the odds are that visitors
from Alpha Centauri will be friendly?

The truth is as terrible as death;
if by "death" we mean
the fear of never waking.

For who knows whether the human spirit
goes up and the spirit of animals
goes down into the earth?

Or with the Sibyl of the Sunday Supplement,
which of our questions
are even worth asking.

Stew

When the voodoo in our hearts
slips from our lips

and drops south to our hands
with all the comic deviltry

of a Celebrity Divorce
or an angel farting in Breughel's hell,

we spy the universe snarling
with its crooked teeth.

And who, pray tell, should apologize
because the world is the way it is

or The Almighty not a bartender
to whom we pray for a good pour?

Eve in the backyard, our loving helpmeet,
lately a snapping turtle in the toilet bowl,

tired of being on the receiving end.
Whilst in our empty Garden,

a sweet breeze teases seeds
from fallen fruit

with two snakes slithering away;
the one that hurts you,

and *yea verily,* the other one—
the one that makes you

hurt yourself.

Psalm 152
    (A Song of Ascent)

Dying of Parkinson's
my mother's handwriting
grew smaller.

As if determined
to erase themselves,
the words conspired
to see what late crumbs
could be shaken loose.

How at the end
her mind faltered,
          grounded
like an engineless plane
or a misbehaving child;

and lovely Lois
got mean,

the kindness stuttered
right out of her,
    a resentful tremolo,

too old and far gone
to renege on any deal,

neither continent
nor competent to choose—

       the microscopic postcard
of her life
not even worth
the stamp it took
to mail it.

And mistaking me
for my dead father,
            complained
about their sex life,
the loss of her studio,
and her inability to paint—

not to mention
the ingratitude
            of her children.

And how God,
like an inattentive husband,
half-listening, had yawned
at her Fred Astaire lamentation

the way sleepers on waking
rub their eyes,
            rollover,
and go back to sleep

It was no substitute, her prayers,
for the real thing;
like an alcoholic's
            sparkling water,

it only pointed
to the greater loss.

Like my poor father, predeceased.
Glad, I'm sure,
to finally be rid of himself—
his catheter snaked
            into the darkest corners
of his bladder,

a urological Frankenstein
                cobbled together
from mismatched bits
of a jigsawed stomach,

haunted by the shadow of a tumor
large enough for a radiologist
to tell time by—

grateful, I'm sure,
for the whole mess
to go up in smoke
        like one of his cheap cigars.

My parents
sparred for 65 years,
familiarly and without ceasing.

Their rope-a-dope marriage
went the distance—
        a draw by any honest referees'
reckoning.

To love, I learned from them,
is to contend
        even to the bitter end.

Bookended now,
they can have their barbed colloquies
without rancor
                and in peace.

At last a meeting of two hearts,
    two minds,

           blended perfectly.

He in one cool corner
of their columbarium niche;

she wedged, quite comfortably,
in the other.

A Hangover with Emily D

I will not drink.
I will not smoke.
The good that I would be,
Moves everywhere but where it should,
Truth framed elliptically.

The life that was,
The life that is,
The good that strangles me:
The fastest way to go to hell
Is go reluctantly.

D.G. "Greg" Geis began working life as a structural welder and worked his way down from there. For twenty-five years he was a portfolio manager for a Swiss bank and Managing Partner for a private investment partnership. Prior to that, he worked in the composing room of a large daily newspaper, as a dude ranch wrangler, a private investigator, sewer man, night shift supervisor of an answering service, TESOL teacher, technical writer, salesman of welding supplies, a taco-bender in a tortilla factory, and for five confusing years, a parish priest.

He has an undergraduate degree in English Literature from the University of Houston and a graduate degree in Philosophy from California State University. Somewhere along the way he also picked up two seminary degrees and a licentiate in philosophical counseling.

He is the author of two previous collections, *Fire Sale* (*Tupleo Press/Leapfolio*) and *Mockumentary* (*Main Street Rag*), and winner of the 2017 Firman Houghton and 2017 Emrys Prizes. His work has appeared in venues as diverse as The Moth, The New Guard, Skylight 47, Crannog, and The Irish Times.

He homesteads twenty acres off the grid in the arid mountains of Central Texas, nursing rocks, cacti, and cedar back to the pink of health.

www.ingramcontent.com/pod-product-compliance
Lightning Source LLC
LaVergne TN
LVHW041552070426
835507LV00011B/1061